LEARNING FROM THE STONES:
A *GO* APPROACH TO
MASTERING CHINA'S STRATEGIC CONCEPT, *SHI*

David Lai

May 2004

FOREWORD

Most of the ideas that form of the foundation of American defense policy and military strategy today were once new and untested concepts at the far edge of strategic thought. It took thinkers of vision and creativity to give them life and refine them to the point they could be adopted by the defense community and used for strategy and force development. This is a never ending process: new strategic concepts constantly emerge, some fade away, a few pass the tests of suitability, feasibility, and acceptability and make it into the mainstream.

To help with this process of identifying those new and untested strategic concepts that merit further examination, the Strategic Studies Institute is publishing a special series called "Advancing Strategic Thought." This provides a venue--a safe haven--for creative, innovative, and experimental thinking about national security policy and military strategy.

The following study by David Lai is the inaugural publication in the Advancing Strategic Thought Series. In it, Dr. Lai uses the ancient game of *Go* as a metaphor for the Chinese approach to strategy. He shows that this is very different than the linear method that underlies American strategy. By better understanding *Go*, Lai argues, American strategists could better understand Chinese strategy.

The Strategic Studies Institute is pleased to officer this unique and creative analysis as part of the Advancing Strategic Thought Series.

DOUGLAS C. LOVELACE, JR.
Director
Strategic Studies Institute

BIOGRAPHICAL SKETCH OF THE AUTHOR

DAVID LAI is on the faculty of the U.S. Air War College. He earned his Ph.D. in Political Science from the University of Colorado in 1997. Dr. Lai's teaching and research interests are in international relations theory, war and peace studies, comparative foreign policy, Asian security affairs, and Chinese politics. He has published widely in his teaching and research subject areas and is currently writing on issues related to the China-Taiwan question, U.S.-Asian relations, and Chinese strategic thinking.

SUMMARY

Most U.S. political and military leaders are aware of the difference in strategic thinking and international behavior between the United States and China. Many have also studied Sun Tzu's *Art of War* and can recite the Chinese master strategist's famous saying: "Know the enemy and know yourself, in a hundred battles you will never be in peril." However, few really understand the essence of the difference.

The author introduces a new approach to learning about the different ways of strategic thinking and interaction in Chinese culture. It is through learning the Chinese board game called *go*. This game is a living reflection of Chinese philosophy, culture, strategic thinking, warfare, military tactics, and diplomatic bargaining. The author also sheds light on the remarkable connection between *go* and the strategic concepts in Sun Tzu's *Art of War*.

A modest claim is made in this writing that a little knowledge of *go* will take U.S. leaders a long way in understanding the essence of the Chinese way of war and diplomacy.

LEARNING FROM THE STONES:
A *GO* APPROACH TO MASTERING CHINA'S
STRATEGIC CONCEPT, *SHI*

In its July 2002 report to Congress, the China Security Review Commission states, "Chinese strategic thinking and military planning differ markedly from our own, underscoring the need to study such differences more carefully." The report also warns "the possibilities of miscalculation, miscommunication, and misunderstanding are high, given the substantial differences in each country's thinking and planning, and require far more attention from U.S. policymakers and the Congress."[1]

Coincidentally the Department of Defense (DoD) also released its annual report on Chinese military power in July 2002. The Pentagon report calls attention to several knowledge gaps in the U.S. understanding of China's strategic thinking. Particularly, it mentions a concept, *shi*, putatively a strategy China uses to exploit the "strategic configuration of power" to its advantage and maximize its ability to preserve its national independence and develop its comprehensive national power. The Pentagon report notes:

> There is no Western equivalent to the concept of "*shi*." Chinese linguists explain it as "the alignment of forces," the "propensity of things," or the "potential born of disposition," that only a skilled strategist can exploit to ensure victory over a superior force. Similarly, only a sophisticated assessment by an adversary can recognize the potential exploitation of "*shi*."[2]

Indeed, *shi* is such an important concept that Sun Tzu, the Chinese grand master of military strategy, uses it for the title of a chapter in his *Art of War*, the world's oldest military treasure.[3] In this chapter, Sun Tzu has discussed four key aspects of *shi*. First, it is the idea of *qi* and *zheng*. *Zheng* is the regular way of doing things, or in military terms, the regular order of battle. A commander deploys troops in regular (*zheng*) ways. However, the commander must mobilize his troops to engage the enemy in extraordinary (*qi*) ways. *Zheng* is, in essence, a given. It is open knowledge to friends and foes. Yet *qi* is a variable and its variation inexhaustible. The second aspect of *shi* is about creating an overwhelming force with irresistible unleashing power (a grindstone against eggs, and the strike of a hawk at its prey). The third aspect of *shi* is about developing a favorable situation with great potential to achieve the political objectives. Finally, *shi* is about taking and maintaining the initiative. As Sun Tzu puts it, "those skilled at making the enemy move do so by creating a situation to which he must conform."

These aspects of *shi* are also found in Sun Tzu's discussion of other key concepts in the *Art of War* such as deception, stratagem, intelligence, deterrence, and so on. Sun Tzu maintains that these key concepts are vital to victory; one must study and master them during peacetime; and it will be too late to consult experts (books or specialists) when grave occasions arise. In essence, Sun Tzu suggests that national leaders, political and military alike, make strategic thinking and employment of tactical skills part of their second nature.

How does one nurture this second nature? Learning and practice are the ways to go. The author offers a new approach to learn and practice Sun Tzu's strategic and operational ideas—through learning the game of *go*.[4] *Go* is of Chinese origin and is the world's oldest board game, yet still remarkably popular and viable. It is probably the most sophisticated game as well. This game bears striking resemblance to the Chinese way of war and diplomacy. Its concepts and tactics are living reflections of Chinese philosophy, strategic thinking, stratagems, and tactical interactions. This game, in turn, influences the way Chinese think and act. This work brings to light another important feature of this game—its connection to the Chinese military classics. The four key aspects of *shi* in Sun Tzu's *Art of War* are also guiding principles of *go*.

In the American culture, many liken the American way of war and diplomacy to the games of chess (power-based fight), poker (bluffing and risk-taking), boxing (force on force), and American football (in many ways, resembles the American war machine). The game of *go* is different from chess, poker, boxing, and American football in many key aspects. While the American way of war has its strengths, a little knowledge and experience of the game of *go* will be a valuable addition to the American political and military wisdom; and it will take U.S. political and military leaders a long way in understanding the Chinese way of war and diplomacy.

CHINESE WAY OF WAR AND DIPLOMACY

A popular saying in the Chinese diplomatic and defense communities is about the Chinese way of war and diplomacy and its difference to that of the West: Chinese place heavy emphasis on strategy and stratagems whereas the West relies more on overwhelming force and advanced capability. By many accounts, this is an accurate characterization. The Chinese even go so far to call China the birthplace of stratagems. After all, China has the world's first comprehensive military classic, the *Art of War*, and the largest number of ancient military writings. While these military writings address many aspects of military affairs, they all emphasize strategy and stratagems.

Among these military classics, Sun Tzu's *Art of War* is undoubtedly the epitome of the Chinese way of war and diplomacy. In this work, Sun Tzu expounds on many key thoughts on warfare and the conduct of war. Three of them are of great significance: a broad conception of the art of war, an emphasis on strategy and stratagem, and a dialectic view on the way to fight.

In the *Art of War*, Sun Tzu treats the political, diplomatic, and logistical preparation for war, war fighting, and the handling of the aftermath of war as integral parts of the art of war. In this broad framework, the art of war is, in essence, the process of diplomacy; war fighting is only diplomacy by other means.

Sun Tzu's emphasis on strategy and stratagems follows from his prudent view on war—it is a vital matter of the state, survival or ruin. Sun Tzu is especially cautious on the cost of war—while waging war can advance a state's interest, it can bring a state disaster as well. As an old Chinese saying goes, when you kill 10,000 enemy soldiers, you are likely to lose 3,000 lives as well. Hence, as Sun Tzu puts it, a farsighted ruler thinks about warfare carefully; a good commander exploits the art of war fully; if there is no benefit, advantage, or real danger, a state must not set the war machine in motion. "Thus those unable to understand the dangers inherent in employing troops are equally unable to understand the advantageous ways of doing so." Preserving the vital interest of a state without the use of force therefore is the first principle in Sun Tzu's *Art of War*. To achieve this goal, Sun Tzu places great emphasis on strategy and stratagems. Thus in the *Art of War*, Sun Tzu treats warfare, from its preparation to execution and termination as first and foremost a contest of wisdom. Use of force is secondary. From Sun Tzu's perspective, a winning side uses force to consolidate assured victory, whereas a losing side uses force only to make a gamble or a desperate attempt for survival, neither of which is a good strategy of war.

Adding complexity to the battle of wits is Sun Tzu's remarkably sophisticated dialectic view on nature, warfare, strategy, and stratagem. The *Art of War* is full of observations about the dialectic nature of strategic concepts such as weak vs. strong, more vs. few, defense vs. offense, regular vs. extraordinary (*qi* and *zheng*), direct vs. indirect, division vs. unity, laboring vs. resting, advance vs. retreat, far vs. near, and the relativity and mutual transformation of these strategic situations. Sun Tzu's teaching is to exploit the opposite of the enemy's strategy and action.

> Therefore, when capable, feign incapacity; when active, inactivity. When near, make it appear that you are far away; when far away, that you are near. Offer the enemy a bait to lure him; feign disorder and strike him. When he concentrates, prepare against him; where he is strong, avoid him. Anger his general and confuse him. Pretend inferiority and encourage his arrogance. Keep him under stress and wear him down. When he is united, divide him. Attack when he is unprepared; sally out when he does not expect you.

Sun Tzu's dialectic views are in complete harmony with the philosophies of *Yin* and *Yang* and Daoism. Sun Tzu and Lao Tzu, the intellect of the Daoist School of thought, particularly liken the character of the military and the way of war and diplomacy to the flow of water. Water is perhaps the best example of the dialectic nature of things. It has no constant shape. There is nothing softer and weaker than water, yet nothing is more penetrating and capable of attacking the hard and strong. The flow of water, carrying with it the *shi*, can wash away anything standing in its way.

With over 2,000 years of influence from Sun Tzu's teaching, along with the influence of other significant philosophical and military writings, the Chinese are particularly comfortable with viewing war and diplomacy in comprehensive and dialectic ways and acting accordingly. Indeed, many of these observations have become proverbial components of the Chinese way of war and diplomacy. The most notable ones are *bing yi zha li* (war is based on deception), *shang-bing fa-mou* (supreme importance in war is to attack the enemy's strategy), *qi-zheng xiang-sheng* (mutual reproduction of regular and extraordinary forces and tactics), *chu-qi zhi-sheng* (win through unexpected moves), *yin-di zhi-sheng* (gain victory by varying one's strategy and tactics according to the enemy's situation), *yi-rou ke-gang* (use the soft and gentle to overcome the hard and strong), *bishi ji-xu* (stay clear of the enemy's main force and strike at his weak point), *yi-yu wei-zhi* (to make the devious route the most direct), *hou-fa zhi-ren* (fight back and gain the upper hand only after the enemy has initiated fighting), *sheng-dong ji-xi* (make a feint to the east but attack in the west), and so on. All of these special Chinese four-character proverbs are strategic and dialectic in nature. All bear some character of flowing water.

This Chinese way of war and diplomacy is in striking difference to the Western way of war from ancient Greece to the United States today. In the Western tradition, there is a heavy emphasis on the use of force; the art of war is largely limited to the battlefields; and the way to fight is force on force. As one observer puts it, "the Greeks developed what has been called the Western way of war—a collision of soldiers on an open plain in a magnificent display of courage, skill, physical prowess, honor, and fair play, and a concomitant repugnance for decoy, ambush, sneak attacks, and the involvement of noncombatants." With respect to stratagem, Alexander the Great said, when he was advised to launch a surprise night attack against the Persians:

> The policy which you are suggesting is one of bandits and thieves, the only purpose of which is deception. I cannot allow my glory always to be diminished by Darius' absence, or by narrow terrain, or by tricks of night. I am resolved to attack openly and by daylight. I choose to regret my good fortune rather than be ashamed of my victory.[5]

The Western way of war finds its comprehensive theoretical expressions in the Western military classics of Carl von Clausewitz and Baron Antoine-Henri de Jomini. It has also made its impressive footprints in battlefields throughout the ages and across the globe. Today, the American way of war has become a more popular term for the Western way of war. As described by military historian Russell F. Weigley, the American way of war uses massive power, excels in advanced technology, and pursues total victory.[6] Backed by U.S. mighty military power, the American way of war has put on impressive shows in wars in Iraq, the former Yugoslavia, and Afghanistan. In the most recent war on Iraq, the 2003 Operation IRAQI FREEDOM, the United States used a "leaner force" (smaller in number as compared to the massive buildup against Iraq in 1991), yet faster in maneuver, armed with sharper precision firepower, and advanced with surprise attacks. Some observers call this revolution in the Western way of war.[7] However, one can see that the fundamentals of the Western way of war remain unaltered. The revolution has only made it more powerful.

Comparing the Chinese and Western ways of war and diplomacy, one cannot but wonder which one is better. The Chinese believe their strategic traditions are superior to those of the West, both ethically and effectively. Chinese strategists tend to stress the significance of culture and end up stereotyping U.S. and Western ways of war.[8] While a good answer to this question is difficult to qualify, one has to see that the West has dominated world politics with its superior comprehensive power over several centuries. The Chinese are aware of this fact. They also understand that without solid and credible capability, the play of strategy is empty. That is why the Chinese are so determined to develop China's comprehensive national power.

That said, one must see that while the Chinese are doing their homework (developing their capabilities), the West should spend some time learning about Chinese strategic thought and stratagem skills. As Sun Tzu puts it, "know your opponent and know yourself, in a hundred battles you will never be in peril."

LESSONS FROM THE GAME OF *GO*

In many ways, the game of *go* resembles the Chinese way of war and diplomacy. This game has its origin in China about 4,000 years ago and is the oldest board game in the world. The original Chinese name of this game is called *weiqi* (pronounced wei ch'i); literally, encircling territory, an essential component of a nation state. Two players compete for territories. The one who acquires more wins.

The game board is conceived to be the earth (back in ancient times, people believed the earth was flat and square). The board is square, representing stability (See Figure 1). The four corners represent the four seasons, indicating the cyclical change of time. The game pieces, the stones, are round, hence mobile. The spread of stones on the board reflect activities on earth. The shape of the stone engagements on the board is like the flow of water, an echo in Sun Tzu's view that the positioning of troops be likened to water: "as water varies its flow according to the fall of the land, a military varies its method of gaining victory according to the enemy situations." Sun Tzu also uses stones to describe military affairs: rolling boulders create *shi*.

The two players take turns to place black and white stones on the intersections (but not the open squares) of a 19 x 19 line matrix, one piece at a time. The black and white stones engage with one another in the game, exemplifying the concept of *yin* and *yang* and penetrating each other's territories as the flow of water.

Figure 1.

The stones have equal physical power (there is no almighty queen or little pawn as in chess), resembling the relatively equal physical size of individuals. Yet the importance and potential of the stones in the game are beyond imagination, resembling the boundless creativity of human individuals. Even a super computer today cannot map out their alternatives. Of note here is that in 1997, the IBM super computer Deep Blue finally defeated the chess grand master Garry Kasparov. Yet at the celebration ceremony, the designers of Deep Blue also admitted that they could not write a program to beat even a mediocre *go* player, not any time soon.

The game of *go* starts with the game board completely open. This special design allows for creative strategic thinking and interaction. By game rule, the one who plays Black goes first. Once played, the stones stay in place unless captured *and* removed by the opposing player. The game will become more complicated as the two players put more stones on the board (unlike chess, where the further the game goes, the fewer pieces on the board, hence simpler).

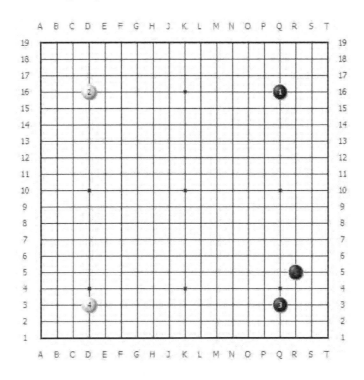

Figure 2.

The basic objective of the game is to secure more space on the board (or more territory). The players do so by encircling more space on the board. The competition for more territory thus leads to invasion, engagement, confrontation, and war fighting. Sun Tzu's thoughts and the essential features of the Chinese way of war are all played out in the game. As the game unfolds, it becomes a war with multiple campaigns and battlefronts. Or in terms of international affairs, it is a competition between two nations over multiple interest areas.

Figure 2 shows the initial five moves of a game between two Chinese professional players.[9] In the game of *go*, the first 50- some moves are called the opening-stage moves. At this point, players develop their strategic plans, adjusting constantly to the new situation created by the opponent's countermoves. Strategic moves, diplomatic posturing, and testing each other's waters are the hallmarks of the opening of the game. These early moves set the stage for the entire game, affecting the battles and campaigns 50 to a 100 moves later and throughout the game (long-term and calculated strategy is a key aspect of this game).

Black 3 and 5 have created a firm command of the corner, securing a "theater" in the lower right side of the war plain. Working in concert with Black 1 at the top, the three black stones make a large claim of "sphere of influence" on the right side of the board.

White must respond to Black's claim. But at this early stage with only a few stones on the board, it is difficult to locate the "center of gravity" or "decisive point" (in Clausewitz and Jomini's terms, respectively). Sun Tzu's teaching to attack your opponent's strategy comes into play. In Figure 3 we see that White immediately placed stone 6 on the board to counter Black's posturing. White 6 instantly changed the *strategic outlook* on the board. The three white stones in turn have made a much larger claim of sphere of influence on the left-hand side. Both players have tried to develop an advantageous situation that is consistent with Sun Tzu's third aspect of *shi*.

Black did not let White's claim stay long. Black 7 struck deep into White's claimed sphere of influence. It went also as an attack on White's strategy (Sun Tzu's teaching), interrupting White's strategic outlook instantly (Figure 4).

Black 7, however, is a very subtle move. It engages White 4 but does not pose a life-threatening situation to White. It is in White's claimed sphere of influence but keeps an arm's length from White 4. At its position, Black 7's strategic potentials are open to imagination. This is a move of long-term and calculated strategic interest.

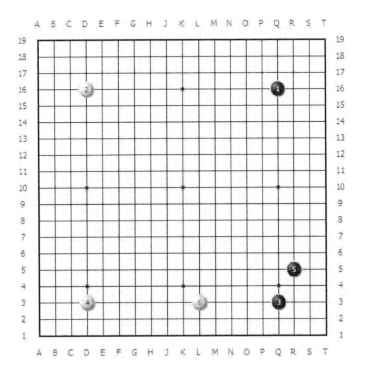

Figure 3.

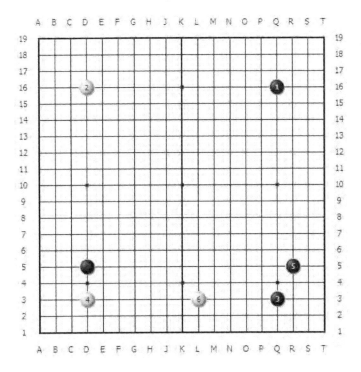

Figure 4.

Black 7 is a typical *go*-style engagement, one that serves to test White's intention (whether White wants to keep the corner or compete for the center). It is also characteristic of the Chinese calculated strategic thinking and behavior. One Chinese act in the 1960s is a good example. During the 1960s, China made much effort to solicit African support for its quest to become a member of the United Nations (UN) (African countries formed a large voting block at the UN General Assembly). One of the Chinese efforts was to build sports stadiums in many African countries. This seemingly unconnected act went a long way to help China get the African votes at the UN (China won the fight and became a UN member in 1971).

The thought and play on Black 7, however, is rather uncharacteristic of American mindset and behavior. Generally, Americans are more straightforward. When Americans take action, they expect immediate return. U.S. policy toward North Korea, for instance, emphasizes reciprocity. Because quick and desirable response from North Korea is difficult to obtain, U.S. decision makers often feel frustrated and tend to see their policy as a failure. South Korea, however, pursues a Sunshine policy toward the North. This policy takes its title from an Aesop fable about "The Sun and the Wind."[10] It counts on long-term and gradual efforts to promote change in North Korea. Americans, not surprisingly, have no patience for such a policy. South Korean leaders in the last several years have been calling on the United States to show more patience and understanding towards their Sunshine policy. Unfortunately, both are in short supply on the American side.

A play like Black 7, which promises no immediate and concrete response from White, is difficult for Americans to make. But this game offers Americans the opportunity to nurture such sensibilities.

In Figure 5 we see that the two players have exchanged a few directly engaged moves. These are standard moves in a situation like this (in Sun Tzu's terms, they are regular engagements, *zheng* moves; and in *go*, they are, *joseki*).

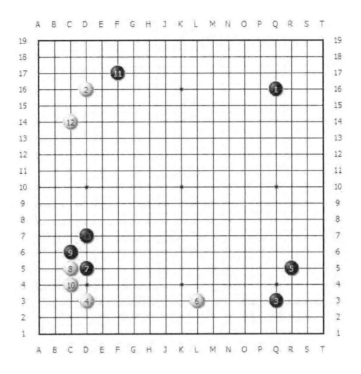

Figure 5.

Consistent with the subtle thought on Black 7, these early engagements are not for the kill, but a testing of the other's reaction and intention. White reinforced his hold on the corner. Black took an outward posturing. The two players exchanged messages: White went after tangible interest (territory) in the corner; Black created a *shi* to pursue interest in the center.

This is also a "live and let live" play. Both are satisfied with the outcome. There has been much writing in Japan about this kind of engagement. The Japanese compare this engagement to the competition for market share between firms.[11] In *go*, as well as in business, it is difficult to have all the gains and profits. Although there is a natural tendency for one to seek landslide victory, a player should guard against this temptation and be prepared to settle with a win-win outcome. Overly aggressive usually leads to disaster.

Black troops 7, 9, and 13 have formed a creative stronghold. This group of three has room to make a secure base along the left-hand side, making this group invincible and able to expand into the center (a good implementation of Sun Tzu's strategy: you must first make yourself invincible and then wait for the enemy to show signs of vulnerability and launch an attack from your secured base).

Black 11 took the initiative to engage White 2 on the upper left-hand corner. Now the reader should look at the overall situation as shown in Figure 5 (looking at the whole picture is a typical Chinese way of assessment). Black's strategic design is clearly on the center and the right side of the war plain. The four groups of Black stones stand in dynamic echoing positions. A promising strategic design is taking shape. Yet it is still premature for Black to celebrate victory at this moment. Indeed, White is waiting for every turn to frustrate Black's strategy. The two white stones 2 and 12 are already eyeing the open area in the center. White 6 at the bottom occupies a critical strategic position. It keeps White's reach into the center wide open. This is a critical countermeasure White made at the early stage of the game against Black's strategic design. Its potential grows as the game unfolds.

At this point, one can say that the two players score fairly in their opening-stage strategic designs. Black has a secured corner on the lower right-hand side. White's countermeasure is a similar sized corner on the lower left-hand side. White 2 and 12 hold part of the upper left-hand corner. Black 11 is waiting for the right moment to penetrate into the corner. Therefore it is a shared claim on the upper left-hand side. On the upper right-hand corner, Black 1 occupies a key strategic position. However, there are wide-open areas on its two sides, making Black's claims vulnerable to challenge from White. During *go* games, players constantly make this kind of assessment till the end.

Figure 6 shows a well-matched engagement between the two players. White 14 has strengthened White 6's strategic claim at the bottom and reinforced White's determination to compete for the center (or to frustrate Black's strategy for the center). At the upper right-hand side theater, White has successfully made an invasion deep into Black's claimed area. Black fought back and effectively separated the white troops into two unconnected groups, while securing its hold on the corner. This is a perfect example of divide and rule, another key feature of *go*. The two white groups have room to maneuver and secure a foothold for survival locally. However, at this moment, they are still vulnerable to attacks from Black.

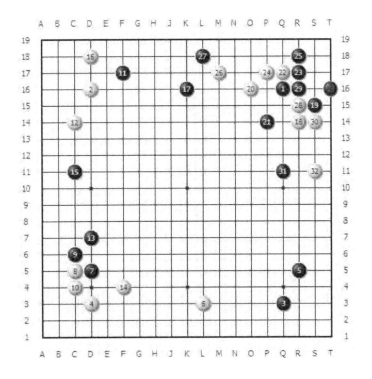

Figure 6.

Of note is another key feature in the game of *go*—the relativity of offense and defense. In Figure 6, while the three Black groups focus on attacking the two White groups, from the left, in the middle, and from the right, the three Black stones at the top (11, 17, and 27) are under a pincer attack from the White groups on their left and right. Who is attacking whom? It is a matter of perspective.

In Figure 7 we see the battle over the fate of the White groups at the top turned bloody. The line of Black troops 21, 43, 45, 53, 49, 39, and 57 threatens the survival of the White group. The battle hinges upon a fight over a *ko* at the intersection of M-14.

Ko is a unique feature. There is no equivalent in other board games. Here is how it comes about and affects the course of the game. The last move on the board is Black's 57. This play removed a White stone from the intersection M-14. By playing this move, Black 57 immediately finds itself surrounded tightly by the three White stones 42, 44, and 46. White can recapture the intersection by removing Black 57. However, this recapturing will then result in an endless play of capture and recapture between the two players. To avoid such a vicious circling play, *go* creates the concept of *ko* and sets a rule that White cannot immediately recapture Black 57, but must make a move elsewhere and give Black a chance to decide if 1) he wants to close the *ko* by filling the intersection with another black stone, or 2) if he wants to respond to White's move elsewhere, allowing White to recapture the *ko* at the next move. In fighting for the *ko*, a player's move elsewhere is always a threat to the opponent's other battle group or territory bigger or equal to the one under siege in the *ko*. As such, the opponent is compelled to respond to the threat, unwillingly allowing the player to recapture the *ko*. The threats are explicit and measurable. It is a fair bargaining game.

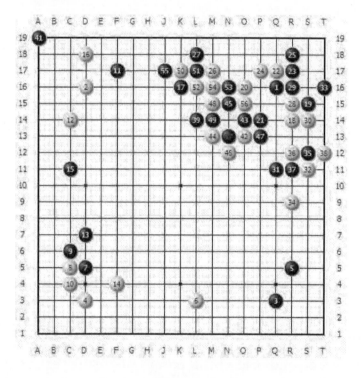

Figure 7.

This aspect of *ko* can shed some light on the U.S. failure to get China to come to terms with the U.S. demand on changes in China's human rights conduct in order to have its most-favored nation (MFN) trade status continued during the 1990s. Three problems made the U.S. threat a failure. First, human rights conduct covers a wide range of issues. It was difficult to single out changes and relate the cost of failing to make such changes to the cost of losing MFN. Second, and making the all-encompassing concept of human rights conduct worse, the United States kept moving the goal post; that is, the changes it wanted China to make. Finally, a termination of MFN cut both ways—China and the United States were both losers if MFN was discontinued. The *ko* in this case was not well-established. The result was that the United States continued to make ill-defined threats; China continued to show defiance; and the MFN continued to be renewed every year.

The *ko* in Figure 7 is well-established. The stakes are clear and high for White. In winning the *ko*, Black would capture the entire White group on the upper side, turning the huge upper side into Black territory. Black could then easily expand this victory into the center. White would have to throw in the towel and concede defeat. For White, this *ko* is a life and death situation, a must-win fight.

In Figure 8 we see that White played 58 at the top, a move that threatens the two Black stones 51 and 27. Black responded with 59, keeping the two White stones under Black's control. If Black does not respond to White's threat (White 58) but chooses to close the *ko*, White will capture the two Black stones 51 and 27. This result will allow White to make a secured garrison at the upper side. If this scenario happens, the Black stones to the left of the White garrison, Black 11, 55, and 17, will be in danger. This is clearly not Black's intent to start this *ko*—Black wanted to profit from this bargaining.

After the exchange between 58 and 59, White turned around to recapture the *ko* by removing Black 57 and placing White 60 into the intersection. It is now Black's turn to make a move elsewhere to continue this *ko*. In Figure 9 we see that Black played 61 (close to the edge on the right). White did not respond to Black's threat to the White group on the right, but chose to eliminate the *ko* by playing 64 at the top to remove the two Black stones 45 and 53. In so doing, White has saved the White group at the top and gained a passage to the center through White stone 60 (resembling a canal). The White troops 42, 44, and 46 are now free of the death threat and are ready to fight in concert with the White troops at the bottom for the open area in the center.

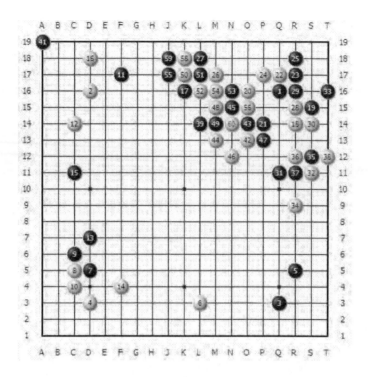

Figure 8.

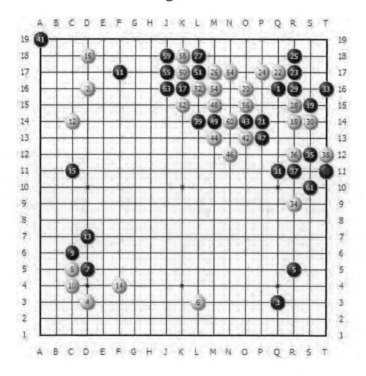

Figure 9.

Black followed through with the *ko* threat to remove White 32 by playing Black 65 (on the intersection S-11). In so doing, the line of Black troops 31, 37, 61, 65, and 35 has trapped the five White stones 36, 38, 18, 28, and 30 inside Black's encirclement (they are now prisoners inside Black's territory). White paid a heavy price for the *ko*. The loss of the White group on the right-hand side has become a huge expansion of Black's territory from the upper right corner to a large portion of the right-hand side. At the same time, White 34 has become helplessly isolated. This situation has a remarkable resemblance to the China-Taiwan case. The *go* concepts can inform us how the mainland Chinese view the Taiwan situation.

From the *go* perspective, one should not try to rescue the lone stone 34. There is not enough space for White to build a survivable garrison around White 34. But if White sends a rescue team to reconnect with 34, Black will attack this rescue team from both sides. In doing so, Black will acquire more territory through the offense. The most sensible strategy therefore is to play 34 as a bargaining chip in another *ko* situation.

This is exactly what the mainland Chinese believe the United States has been doing with Taiwan throughout the years—it is a leverage to hold against China from time to time. This is also what China tells Taiwan: you are only a bargaining chip on a *go* board (or a pawn in the U.S. chessboard).

However, Taiwan has also been a liability for the United States—it carries the risk of involving the United States in an armed conflict with mainland China over the fate of Taiwan. From the *go* perspective, many Chinese would ridicule Americans for their lack of understanding of this geo-strategic situation between Taiwan and mainland China—it is a lone stone against a huge mass. The United States, believing in its ability to project power in the Western Pacific, nevertheless dismisses China's view. However, the cost of defending Taiwan must not be underestimated. The *go* perspective provides a theoretical and strategic insight into the costs.

Returning to the game here, we see that Black took advantage of the huge *shi* from the upper side, and working in concert with the stronghold of Black 3 and 5 at the bottom, launched a campaign to expand into the center from the right.

The closure of the *ko* also concluded the first mid-game battle. Black was a clear winner in this first fight. In an attempt to turn this disadvantage around, White made an advance at the bottom with White 66. This move has expanded White's territory at the bottom. It also posed a threat to the Black stronghold of 3 and 5. This move also signified the start of the second mid-game battle in a separate theater.

Black answered White's threat by reinforcing the stronghold and building a "wall" with stones 3, 77, 5, 73, 79, 87, and 89. Through these efforts, Black has effectively consolidated the control on the entire right-hand side. The two White stones 34 and 82 have become captives.

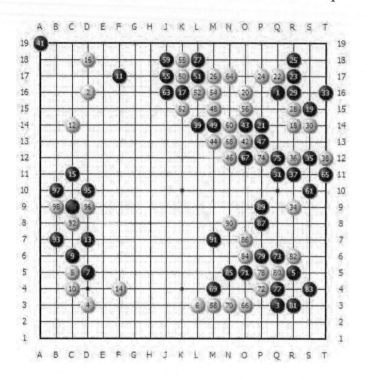

Figure 10.

White, however, was able to reinforce the hold at the bottom part (with white stones 66, 70, 88, and 6 lining up a border). During the engagement, the two players have both separated a portion of the other's troops from the main forces (divide and rule). The three baseless White 84, 86, and 90 are trying to reconnect with the White group in the middle. The Black troops 71, 85, 69, and 91, however, are in a different mindset. They worked in concert with the Black troops 87 and 89 to chase the fleeing White troops. This is clearly an example of "the best defense is offense." While attacking the fleeing White group, Black 91 also occupies a key strategic position to reconnect with the Black group on the left if it is under attack.

This situation shows a key aspect of warfare—the *yin* and *yang* and relativity of defense and offense.

With Black 91 on the board, the second mid-game battle came to a truce. The two players then turned to the left side and started another mid-game battle. As shown in Figure 10, the two opponents have started another *ko* battle. This *ko* holds the fate of the two groups, Black 16, 95, and 97 on one side and White 92, 96, and 98 on the other. From *go* players' experience, whoever wins this *ko* wins the game.

In Figure 11 we see that Black has captured a fairly large portion of the center. Black has also captured the fleeing White 84, 86, and 90 and three extra White stones 72, 78, and 80 (those White stones have been removed, leaving the vacated intersections in Black's territory (L-9, L-8, M-8, N-7, N-6, and O-7). Black has obviously gotten more territory out of the fight over the *ko*.

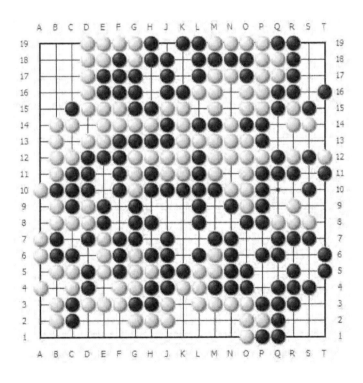

Figure 11.

In Figure 12, those "dead" stones are removed to provide a better view of the settled territories. The borders are all sealed. These irregular lines of border happen to look like real-world national borders. We see that Black has the entire right-hand side territory. This black territory then expands into the center area. There is a self-sustained black territory at the top. The sum of these areas is Black's hard-earned territory (the borders and open space inside inclusive.)

White has the left-hand side, but it is narrower than Black's territory on the right. White also has about two-thirds of the bottom side. In addition, White has a self-sustained group on the upper middle part.

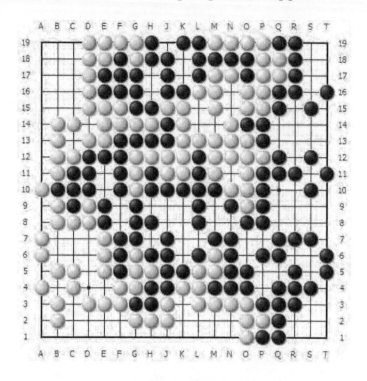

Figure 12.

There are two ways to count the points. One is the Japanese way that counts the open intersections inside one's secured territory. The other is the Chinese way of counting all the intersections, occupied and open. The two ways of counting come to the same conclusion. The one who has more points (intersections) wins. In this game, Black won by having 3 3/4 intersections more than White has.

The presentation in this section gives the reader a taste of *go*. It really shows how patient the Chinese are in playing strategic games.

This discussion of the game is focused on the strategic level of engagements. *Go* is very rich in tactical operations as well. Studying and practicing the tactics in local life-and-death situations are equally challenging in *go*. There are many books about *go* in English at all levels nowadays. Interested readers should check out the *American Go Association* web site. You can find the most basic books about *go* and learn about the latest development in *go*-related activities.[12]

SHI IN ACTION

China is home to Sun Tzu. There is also a long tradition of strategic thinking in China. However, this cultural heritage was laid 22 aside during the early turbulent years of the People's Republic. Since China embarked on the mission of national development in 1978, there has been a revival of interest in Sun Tzu and other classical Chinese military thoughts in China. The proliferation of publications in China on studies of classical Chinese military thought and reprints of the original military classics is a good testimony.[13] There is also ample indication that China is following the wisdom of its classical strategic thought to make impressive progress in pursuing its national objectives, particularly the objectives to develop China and retake Taiwan. A noted success in China's strategy is its efforts in creating the *shi* for its missions.

Developing the *Shi* to Secure a Home Base.

In 1978, under the leadership of Deng Xiaoping, Chinese leaders launched the now acclaimed economic reform in China. The Chinese leaders were determined to turn China into a true great power in 50 to 100 years. To achieve this goal, China needs a favorable internal and external environment.

Internally, Chinese leaders follow the model of economic development under authoritarian rule. Externally, they take a three-pronged strategy to create a favorable environment for China's development. First and foremost, Chinese leaders seek a constructive relationship with the United States. Second, they mend fences with China's neighboring countries. Third, they aggressively integrate China into the global community.

In all fairness, this strategy has borne fruit. On the home front, economic reform has reached all corners of China. Chinese government has loosened control on pricing, labor market, housing, and many other areas. A flourishing market economy has taken hold in China. Economic reform has also come to China's financial and banking industries. With its entry to the World Trade Organization (WTO) as a catalyst for bigger changes, China is expected to accelerate its economic reform and become completely integrated into the world market economy.

On the external front, one cannot dismiss China's three-pronged efforts. In the last 10 years, China has gradually built a "ring of friends" around its borders. It has normalized relations with Russia 23 (1991), the Central Asia former Soviet republics (1992), South Korea (1992), Laos (1989), Indonesia (1990), Brunei (1991), Vietnam (1991), and Singapore (1990).

China has also settled border disputes with Laos (complete), Vietnam (all except for the South China Sea islands), Russia (97 percent borders delimited), the three Central Asian former Soviet republics of Kazakstan, Kirgizstan, and Tajikistan (all complete), and stabilized border disputes with India and Bhutan.

Through these internal and external efforts, China has secured a firm home base, and a sound strategic *shi* to pursue its national objectives.

Developing the *Shi* on Taiwan.

Recovering Taiwan is China's historical mission. China's objective is to take Taiwan whole and intact. To achieve this goal, China tries to follow Sun Tzu's teaching to win without resorting to force. Developing the *shi* thus is a critical strategy. This strategy has three components. The first is economic and social integration; the second is to establish a credible deterrence against attempts inside Taiwan to make a desperate run for independence; and the third is to hold the United States committed to the one-China policy.

By many accounts, China has been successful in executing this strategy. Perhaps the biggest achievement of this strategy is in developing the *shi* through the cross-Strait economic and social integration. As the numbers in Table 1 show, since the late 1980s, cross-Strait trade has a cumulative amount of $302.8 billion. According to another Taiwan government statistic, the share of annual cross-Strait trade in Taiwan's total trade has grown from less than 1 percent in 1983 to 15.39 percent in 2002.[14]

China has also attracted a large amount of capital investment from Taiwan. The cumulative sum is over $30 billion from 1991 to 2003. It is 44.53 percent of Taiwan's total foreign investment over this period.

Item	Current Month	Year to Date	Cumulative	Source
The Cross-Strait Indirect Trade	May 2003	Jan-May 2003	1987-May 2003	
Total (U.S. $100 million)	35.4 (12.8%)	172.9 (25.7%)	3,028	Hong Kong
Exports	27.1 (8.4%)		2,527	Customs,
Imports	8.3 (30.1%)		501	Ministry of
Trade Balance	18.8 (0.9%)		2,026	Finance (ROC)
Indirect Investment to Mainland	May 2003	Jan-May 2003	1991-May 2003	
Cases	138 (1.0%)	797 (56%)	30,075*	Investment Commission
Amount (U.S. $100 million)	3.17 (4.0%)	17.34 (44%)	313.1*	Ministry of Economic Affairs (ROC)
Reference Statistics by Mainland		Jan-Mar 2003	1979-Mar 2003	
Projects		1,040	56,731	Ministry of Foreign Trade
Contracted Amount (U.S.$100 million)		16.9	631.6	and Economic Cooperation
Realized Amount (U.S.$100 million)		8.9	340.0	(PRC)
Exchange of Visits	Apr 2003	Jan-Apr 2003	1988-Apr 2003	
Taiwan Visitors Arrivals in Mainland (1,000 persons)	108.5 (-68.4%)	909 8 (-22.0%)	28,144.4	China Monthly Statistics
	May 2003	Jan-May 2003	1988-May 2003	
Mainland People Visit Taiwan	3,654 (-71.0%)	55,544 (-12.3%)	914,600	Bureau of Immigration, Ministry of the Interior (ROC)

Notes: 1. Numbers in () stand for growth rate compared within the same period of the last year.
2. "Taiwan People Visit Mainland" monthly figures are not available since May 2000. The statistics are replaced by "Taiwan Visitors Arrivals in Mainland" which is from China Monthly Statistics published by China Statistical Information and Consulting Co. Ltd. (Beijing).

Source: Mainland Affairs Council, Executive Yuan, August 7, 2003.

Table 1. Preliminary Statistics of Cross-Strait Economic Relations, May 2003.

Between 1988 and 2003, over 28 million Taiwan visitor entries to the mainland have been recorded. Many Taiwan people, most of them business executives, high-tech gurus, and people with high demand skills, have relocated to the mainland. Shanghai alone has housed over 50,000.

Many factories have also been relocated from Taiwan to the mainland. China has become such a "giant sucking ground" for Taiwan's business, capital, and talented people that Japan's "Mr. Strategy" and business guru, Kenichi Ohmae, predicts that by 2005 Taiwan will have to submit to unification with China. Or, if Taiwan refuses to accept this fate, it will become "Taiwan passing, Taiwan nothing!"[15]

Ohmae's call may sound too demanding. The rapid and large-scale cross-Strait economic and social integration surely suggests a virtual unification is possible in 10 years.

On the military front, China has gradually built up several rings of missiles along its eastern seaboard since the early 1990s. These missiles pose a credible threat to Taiwan. In addition, China has also strengthened its overall air and naval capabilities. This military *shi* has reinforced China's resolve to keep Taiwan in the fold.

On the U.S. front, China has strengthened ties with the United States. The U.S.-China relationship was at low ebb when President Bush took office. It hit an all time low when the two countries found themselves in a standoff over a military aircraft collision on April 1, 2001 (the U.S. EP-3 spy plane and Chinese J-8 fighter jet collision incident over the South China Sea). Later in April 2001, following the release of the 24 EP-3 crew members from China, President Bush authorized a large sale of weapons to Taiwan and promised to "do whatever it takes to help Taiwan defend themselves."[16] Chinese leaders, however, made much effort to reverse the downward trend in the U.S.-China relations afterwards. By July of 2001, China had Secretary of State Colin Powell visit China. Powell was all smiles in Beijing, calling China a friend. Then came the September 11 terrorist attacks on the United States. Chinese leaders jumped on the opportunity to cooperate with the United States in its war against terrorism. With its hands full with heavy involvements in the Middle East and North Korea, the United States clearly values the U.S.-China ties more than distractions from Taiwan. A *shi* is clearly established in China's favor.

Against this backdrop, Taiwan President Chen Shui-bian started to push aggressively for two referendums in Taiwan, one on the issue of a nuclear power plant, and the other on Taiwan's quest to become an observer to the World Health Organization. Although many see these proposed referendums as Chen's attempt to create issues for his reelection in March 2004, the real purpose for is Chen's agenda to have a referendum for Taiwan's formal independence.

This hidden agenda has the potential to trigger an armed conflict in the Taiwan Strait. In the past, China would have taken up the issue with Chen Shui-bian and intensify its threat to use force against Taiwan's attempts. But this time China was looking on with folded arms. The United States was more concerned with this issue. An armed conflict in the Taiwan Strait would involve the United States because of its commitment to

Taiwan's defense through the Taiwan Relations Act of 1979. However, the United States had no desire whatsoever to have an armed conflict with China over Taiwan at this time. Thus as a precaution, U.S. representative to Taiwan Doug Paal (a *de facto* ambassador) expressed concern to Chen. The 26 latter unwillingly had reassured the United States that a referendum on Taiwan independence would not come up in the upcoming presidential election. China did not have to fire missiles this time. Its *shi* was working.

Chen, however, did not give up his efforts. As Taiwan's presidential election campaigns intensified during the final months of 2003, Chen proposed to hold two more referendums on the election day in March 2004 (one "defensive referendum" against China's missile threat and another referendum to amend Taiwan's constitution). Chen's controversial efforts made the United States more concerned. Thus at a joint news conference with the visiting Chinese premier at the White House on December 9, 2003, President George W. Bush bluntly stated that the United States opposed Taiwan's attempt to unilaterally change the status quo of the Taiwan Strait.

Having President Bush take such a clear stand was clearly a score on the Chinese side. However, the Chinese would not just sit back and relax. They continued to maintain the *shi* over the Taiwan issue. As explained by People's Liberation Army (PLA) Lieutenant General, Li Jijun:

> The extensive and profound Chinese culture has nurtured an oriental military science that is unique and has lasting influence. Ancient Chinese military science was one that exalted resourcefulness, stratagem and prudence in waging any war or resorting force. This military culture based on reflecting on war, having evolved from war's primitive form of fighting each other, later reached the stage where a strategist is not a militarist. It showed the beauty of philosophic wisdom. Because of this culture, unification war planners, while structuring their strategies, would follow the principle that, "in drawing up a military strategy, importance should be given to stratagem." The objective was "complete" victory without having to resort to force. To this end, they would comprehensively analyze the strategic situation, carefully structure their strategic policies, set proper strategic objectives, correctly choose their strategic course, specifically plan their strategic moves, and properly employ strategic means.[17]

STONES FROM OTHER HILLS

U.S. political and military leaders are familiar with games such as chess, poker, boxing, and American football. These games to a large extent reflect and in turn influence American culture, strategic thinking, and the American way of war. Former National Security Advisor Zbigniew Brzezinski's thought on *The Grand Chessboard: American Primacy and Its Geostrategic Imperatives* is a prime example.[18]

The common feature of these favorite American games is the centrality of physical force and its application. While these games and the American way of war have much strength, they also have weaknesses. The strong aspect is the American and the West's edge on capability. The weak point is the lack of sophisticated skill on strategy and stratagem. The Chinese way of war and the game of *go* have much to offer in helping the Americans overcome their shortcomings. As a Chinese proverb goes, stones from other hills may serve to polish the jade of this one. American leaders will do themselves a great service in learning about *go* and the Chinese way of war. The following discussion highlights the key features of the American favorite games, their influence on the American way of war, and their differences to *go* and the Chinese way of war.

Chess is a game of power-based competition. Each piece on the chessboard carries different weight—a hierarchy of power and rank reflecting a political and military entity. The outcome of the game can be predicted by counting the pieces and their strength on the board. *Go* is a skill-based game. In the game of *go*, each piece has the same tangible power, but their intangible and potential power, based on the near-infinite combinations and alternative ways of engagement, is situational and limitless. The stones on the board work collectively and always in concert with one another to fight battles. It is difficult to predict victory with a casual look at the individual pieces.

Under the influence of chess with heavy emphasis on capability, Americans tend to pay more attention to the balance of military power in conflict situations. Many conclusions also come from the analysis of military balance. The analysis of military balance across the Taiwan Strait is a prime example. Repeated studies and reports show that China does not currently have sufficient military power to launch an invasion on Taiwan. Some would then dismiss China's threat on Taiwan and encourage Taiwan to pursue its agenda.

Another difference between chess and *go* is in their different designs for committing fighting resources. In chess, all the fighting resources are lined up at the beginning of the war. The two players eliminate each other's resources (pieces) to death. In *go*, the two players start with the battlefields open and then deploy troops in the theaters at the early stage of the game. They initiate a fight here and there at the mid-game stage, constantly making decisions as to where to commit troops and how much more resources (more stones) for such commitments. If they sense a losing battle or that a particular operation is not feasible, they will stop committing more resources there (recall the discussion on the Taiwan example resembling an isolated stone in Figure 11). Thus a chess mindset-guided military analysis focuses on what one can achieve given limited resources at the moment, whereas a *go* player thinks about what he can bring to bear with additional resources.

The philosophy behind chess is to win decisively. For the winner, victory is absolute, as is defeat for the loser. In chess, both players have the same clear and overriding objective—capturing the opposing king—and accomplish this objective by decimating whatever opposing forces are standing in the way. In *go*, total victory usually happens between two mismatched players. That kind of victory, as Sun Tzu puts it, is not the pinnacle of excellence. In a *go* game between two well-matched players, the margin between win and lose is usually very small, often decided by only a few points. The philosophy behind *go* therefore is to compete for relative gain rather than seeking complete annihilation of the opponent forces. It is dangerous to play *go* with the chess mindset. One can become overly aggressive so that he will stretch his force thin and expose his vulnerable parts in the battlefields.

In chess, the focus is on the king. All the moves are geared toward checking the king. In designs to capture the king, chess players always try to eliminate the powerful pieces such as the queen, knight, castle, and bishop. Chess players typically focus on these powerful military units as the "center of gravity" and "decisive point" (in Clausewitz and Jomini's terms). Naturally, chess players are single-minded. In *go*, it is a war with multiple campaigns and battlefields. There is no one single focus on the board. A *go* player must always keep the whole situation in mind. Attacking the opponent's strategy therefore is much more appropriate in *go*. As a prolonged and complex game, *go* players focus on building or creating rather than chess players' emphases on removal and destruction.

Another favorite American game is poker. This game also has strong influence on U.S. foreign policy conduct. The key features of poker are risk-taking and bluffing. Poker players have no control over what appears in their hands. Risk-taking and bluffing therefore are the best strategies to make the most out of the cards in hand. Typical manifestations of poker-type foreign policy are threats and ultimatums. Most of these acts are short-term and gambling approaches. While poker-like international interactions do exist, calculated and long-term-based strategies to achieve foreign policy goals are clearly more important. *Go* is probably the most calculated game in the world. When players put their troops (stones) in uncertain situations, they do so by placing their troops in places where they will have a good fighting strategy to make a foothold locally or reconnect with the home base. Testing water rather than bluffing is the way of *go*. *Go* players set up negotiation as in the case of *ko* but do not utilize a risky ultimatum as in poker.[19]

Still another sport that resembles the U.S. use of force is boxing. Boxing is a fight of hard force on force. Boxers meet incoming punches with punches. The more powerful boxer wins the fight. The Chinese counterpart to boxing is *Taiji Quan* (Tai Chi Chuan). *Taiji* practitioners never meet incoming hits with forceful returns. Instead, they always try to deflect incoming hits and then return with a seemingly soft but powerful push. *Taiji* is perhaps the best example of the Chinese philosophy of *yi-rou ke-gang* (use the soft and gentle to overcome the hard and strong). It is in complete harmony with the philosophies behind *go* and Sun Tzu's *Art of War*.

Finally, American football also embodies the U.S. use of force. Football is a game of intense violence. It has powerful players on the field. Forceful collision known as the tackling is the hallmark of football plays. The running back's quick hitter charging into the line of defense is perhaps the best example of the concentration of forces and the philosophy of force on force competition. U.S. armed forces and their emphasis on the use of overwhelming force greatly resemble American football. As National Security Advisor Condoleezza Rice puts it, American football is deeply embedded in the American psyche of competition; it is the U.S. national pastime and an important American institution. Dr. Rice has made repeated remarks that she would like to become the commissioner of the National Football League after her service at the National Security Council.[20] Indeed, U.S. military has incorporated football terminology in its combat language and vice versa. Football has its "blitz," "trenches," and "bombs," while the U.S. military named some of its tactics in the Persian Gulf War as the "Hail Mary maneuver" and "Operation LINEBACKER" in Vietnam. In the most recent war on Iraq (Operation IRAQI FREEDOM), U.S. commanders used the term "red zone operation" to describe their advance into downtown Baghdad. In Lieutenant General David McKiernan's words, "I came up with the term, 'the red zone,' kind of based on that analogy that, you know, you get inside the 20-yard line and maybe it gets a little harder to move the ball. And you got to pound it out a little bit then."[21]

American football has no "peer competitor." Although the National Football League has tried for years to promote football overseas by having some pre-season games in foreign soils, no other country has been able to adopt this sport. American football does have a counterpart. It is soccer, which has a completely different paradigm of war that relies on skills and maneuvers rather than force on force play. Soccer is also a national game of China. In fact, soccer-like sport also has a long history in China. In many ways, soccer is also a paradigm of Sun Tzu's way of war. It does not seek annihilation of the opponent. Instead, it uses strategies and tactics of surprise, finesse, and continual movement of the ball in attempts to create strategic opportunities for goals.

Another key feature in American football is its clear division between offense and defense. When the team is on offense, the offense lineup is in charge. When the opponents are on the offense, the defense lineup comes in to play. The strategies and plays in offense and defense are completely different. In soccer, *go*, and Sun Tzu's teaching, offense and defense are a dialectic whole. Soccer players constantly switch between offense and defense. In the game of *go*, there is no clear-cut frontline—defense or offense is relative; it is a matter of perspective. Operating in the American football mindset, one is single-minded.[22]

The above comparisons and the analysis in this monograph drive home a point: a clear difference exists between the Chinese 31 and American (Western) ways of war and diplomacy. The question is whether the Chinese way is worth learning. After all, as a popular saying in the West goes, with superior force, a lousy general can win a war. As long as the United States and the West maintain their capability edge, they have nothing to worry about. The answer from this author, as this monograph has built the case, is a resounding yes. This answer stands on three good reasons (and can certainly have more). First, ever since warfare came into being part of human affairs, it has been a contest of physical force as well as wits. In the evolution of warfare, the battle of wits has become more important than the actual use of force to achieve war aims (political goals). Today, we call the battle of wits, "strategy." It is about the ways to use force. The United States is the most powerful country in force capability terms, but less so in resourcefulness. The Chinese way of war and diplomacy can be a great supplement to American power. If one looks at American power as the *yang* (the upfront force) and the Chinese stratagems as the *yin* (the behind-the-scene wits), it is only natural that the two should complement each other. The Chinese are determined to improve their capabilities; Americans should improve their strategies and stratagems.

Second, as Sun Tzu suggests, use of force is only diplomacy by other means; if we only focus on the use of force, we miss a big part of diplomacy. American and Western conception of strategy, in the words of Clausewitz, is "the use of engagement for the object of the war."[23] This focus is inadequate. International politics contains war as well as nonwar interactions. The Chinese way of war and diplomacy will help the United States strengthen its leadership in the whole process of diplomacy.

Finally, it pays to learn about your opponents. The world knows the United States is the most powerful nation in the history of mankind. Other nations also understand that confronting the United States directly is an invitation to defeat and humiliation. How can weaker countries deal with the United States? They will resort to "unrestricted warfare" strategies and tactics. The Chinese way of war and diplomacy is about strategy and stratagems; it is about how one can win from the position of the weak. The two Chinese senior colonels who wrote the controversial book, *Unrestricted Warfare*, followed Sun Tzu's teaching closely to develop their thoughts in this book.[24] Terrorists and weaker powers can employ those unconventional approaches to frustrate the superpower. They can also employ the *go, Taiji*, and soccer strategies to maneuver with the United States. Americans will do themselves a great service to follow Sun Tzu's dictum to learn about the Chinese way of war and diplomacy, and as this writing suggests, learning from the stones is the way to go.

ENDNOTES

[1] China Security Review Commission, *Report to the Congress of the United States*, July 2002.

[2] Secretary of Defense, *Annual Report to the Congress on the Military Power of the People's Republic of China*, July 2002, p. 6. Pentagon's 2003 report reiterates this observation.

[3] The international publishing community is now using the *pinyin* spelling system. This article also follows this new practice. However, I keep the traditional spelling of Sun Tzu in this writing. The quotes from Sun Tzu's *Art of War* are from Samuel B. Griffith's translation, Oxford University Press, 1963, unless footnoted otherwise.

[4] The Chinese name for *go* is *weiqi*, pronounced as *wei ch'i*. Literally, it means a game of encircling territories. Japanese call the game *Igo*, Koreans call it *Baduk*, Americans call this game *Go*, so goes it in the rest of the world.

[5] Roger D. McGrath, "The Western Way of War: From Plato to NATO," *Chronicles: A Magazine of American Culture*, February 2001, pp. 13-15.

[6] Russell F. Weigley, *The American Way of War: A History of United States Military Strategy and Policy*, Bloomington: Indiana University Press, 1973.

[7] Max Boot, "The New American Way of War." *Foreign Affairs*, July/August 2003.

[8] See Andrew Scobell, *China and Strategic Culture*, Carlisle, PA: U.S. Army War College Strategic Studies Institute, 2002. For an articulation of Chinese strategic culture by a leading Chinese military strategist, see Li Jijun, *Traditional Military Thinking and the Defensive Strategy of China*, Letort Paper No. 1, Carlisle, PA: U.S. Army War College Strategic Studies Institute, 1997.

[9] This sample game is taken from Qisheng Daochang, an Internet *weiqi* site *www.tom.com*. It is a national tournament game between two Chinese professional players, Chen Linxin and Zhou Junxun, played on August 7, 2003. Chen played black and won the game by 3 3/4 stones.

[10] "The Wind and the Sun," Edna Johnson, ed., an Aesop's fable in *Anthology of Children's Literature*, Boston: Houghton Mifflin Company, 1959, p. 114.

[11] Miura Yasuyuki, *Go: An Asian Paradigm for Business Strategy*, San Francisco: Ishi Press, 1995.

[12]

[13] A search on the World Book Catalogue through the First Search engine will show the numbers.

[14] Mainland Affairs Council, Republic of China, *www.mca.org*, 2003.

[15] Kenichi Ohmae, *The Emergence of the United States of Chunghwa*, Taipei: Business Weekly Publications, 2002.

[16] Interview with ABC Good Morning America anchor Charles Gibson, April 24, 2001.

[17] Li Jijun, "The Unification Belief of the Chinese Nation," *Liao Wang*, a Beijing-based magazine, December 8, 2003, No. 49, p. 1. Li is a leading PLA figure in the promotion of Chinese strategic culture and the Chinese way of war and diplomacy. His 1997 speech at the U.S. Army War College, which was subsequently published as an Army War College Letort Paper entitled *"Traditional Military Thinking and the Defense Strategy of China,"* stands as a leading publication on China's view on its strategic culture.

[18] New York: Basicbooks, 1997.

[19] See David Lai and Gary W. Hamby, "East Meets West: An Ancient Game Sheds New Light on U.S.-Asian Strategic Relations," *The Korean Journal of Defense Analysis*, Vol. XIV, No. 1, Spring 2002, for an in-depth discussion of the difference between *go*, chess, and poker, and their influences on international relations.

[20] Interview with National Security Advisor Condoleezza Rice, *Sports by Brooks*, April 17, 2002. Rice also made these remarks at the Meet the Press with NBC's Tim Russet.

[21] Interview with CNN, June 29, 2003. Lieutenant General McKiernan was the commander of the Third U.S. Army, a main force in the Operation IRAQI FREEDOM.

[22] See Joel F. Cassman and David Lai, "Football vs. Soccer: American Warfare in an Era of Unconventional Threats," *Armed Forces Journal*, November 2003, for a thought-provoking discussion of the two paradigms of war.

[23] Carl von Clausewitz, *On War*, Michael Howard and Peter Paret, trans., Princeton University Press, 1976, p. 128.

[24] Qiao Liang and Wang Xiangsui, *Unrestricted Warfare: Assumptions on War and Tactics in the Age of Globalization,* Beijing: PLA Literature and Arts Publishing House, 1999.

Printed in Germany
by Amazon Distribution
GmbH, Leipzig